By Leo James
© 2020

Special Message

2020 has been a tough year for us all, but remember to keep faith. Believe that better days are ahead of us. I pray this book will touch your mind, heart, and soul. *The Last Tears* symbolize the recognition and understanding of one's past and present memories. The shed of these tears take the form of sharing. Those shared memories then reflect Love, Pain, and Glory. Those forms are phases we encounter in life from birth to now. Whether you know it or not, your own love, pain, and glory is preparing you to truly understand your purpose on this earth. Remember to be positive and count your blessings every day. Just know that things can always be worse and that there is someone out there in the world going through something worse than you are. Reflect and think about how far you've come and then how far you plan to go. No one or nothing can stop you but YOU. If you can't find anything to be grateful, then listen to yourself breathe. That's a blessing itself, so smile and be happy for yourself. We all know that tomorrow is never promised, so reach out to all of your loved ones and express how much you love and care for them. Enjoy my Love, Pain, and Glory: The Last Tears.

-Love and Blessings,
Leo James

Table of Contents

SPECIAL MESSAGE	2
COUGAR	6
ALONE	7
ALL CRIED OUT	8
BROKEN HEART	9
PROTECTION	10
CHEERS TO SUCCESS	11
HARD PART OF LIFE	12
EYE OPENER	13
PLEASE, THINK!	14
THANKSGIVING	15
BREAK THE CYCLE	16
BELIEVE IN ME	17
11:11	18
LOVE MY SIBLINGS	19
THE VIEW	20
THE AWAKENING	21
FOLLOW MY PATH	22
7,7...	23
DISTANT LOVERS	24
ATTENTION	25
THANK YOU, TOO!	26
DIVORCE OR LIFETIME OF HAPPINESS	27
THE TIME	28
HUG	29
JOURNEY OF WRITER'S BLOCK	30
BORN GENIUS	33
YES, I WILL!	34
THE GHETTO	35
BEING BLACK	36
THE KEY	37
DRIVEN	38
US VS. THEM	40

REAL TALK	41
BLACK SHEEP FROM THE HERD	42
SON OF AN UNDERTAKER	43
HOOD POET	44
UNIFY	45
VENTING	46
THE VOICE	47
REMEMBER	48
PARENTHOOD	49
UNFINISHED BUSINESS	50
BACKWARDS	51
PICK UP THE PIECES	52
THE STRUGGLE	53
WHAT? KEEP!	54
4 ME 2 YOU (DEDICATED TO CLASS OF "09")	55
MEMORY LANE	56
HELPING HAND	57
ANOTHER	58
KARMA	59
F.O.E. (FAMILY OVER EVERYTHING)	60
SOCIAL TRUTH	61
STRESS	62
CONTROLLED	63
BORN-LEADER	64
DIRTY STREETS	65
P.R.E.V.A.I.L PART 3	66
PARANOIA	67
LEFT ON READ/SEEN	68
PRAYING HANDS	69
PURE JEWELS	70
NEW HAVEN (HEAVEN)	71
DREAMS TO REALITY	72
GREATNESS	73
037	74

SPEAKING IT IN2 EXISTENCE 75
NIRVANA 76
MASTERMIND 77
FOR YOU AND ALL YOUTH 78
THE END 79
BREAK UP 2 MAKE UP 80
MOST HIGH 81
BLESSINGS 82
REAL RECOGNIZE REAL 83
20/20 VISION 84
THE LAST TEARS 85

Cougar

These special ladies could be my cougar—
War ready with my eyes on a Ruger.
I touch everything spiritually
That's the way I maneuver.
I love a strong woman with a mindset
like Angela Davis or Assata Shakur
who has an amazing poetic tongue,
like Nikki Giovanni
and Maya Angelou
I would give them this young poetic tongue
with an intelligent head
that would touch their bodies from
head to toe.
We would converse and write for foreplay,
We would act it out all night and day.
Entangle words together as a game
and start it up like,
"Jada would say."
I'm turned on
by the resilient strength
Longevity of prevailing,
I respect the length
So strong that you kept going
You've touched a young man
from my generation
without even knowing.
I just wish I met you amazing ladies
We would have created some amazing
revolutionary
and writing babies,
I'm a caged bird who can really sing,
The "Kidnap Poem"
that's my kind of thing.
Go back and forth with me
like we're on a swing
It wouldn't be an affair
but a writer's fling,
True Queen!
Afrocentric,
I've seen the growth
and power all inside the 'fro,
Fist in the air
Let it fly don't let it go;
You could be my cougar,
not only for us
but for the world to know.

Alone

I've learned how to provide,
protect,
and procreate;
A happy family is something
I've always wanted to create,
Testimony of what I've experienced
is why I'm destined to be great.
I grew up from a boy and became a man,
Trials and tribulations
that some won't understand,
Had to raise a kid
then started paying bills
That thought alone to this day
Still gives me the chills.
Seen my dad do it
so I thought
it wasn't a big deal,
Had to experience it firsthand
to understand how it's real,
Imagine doing all that
and still have to cook and clean,
I still keep a smile on my face
instead of looking mean,
Co-parenting got us both
giving child support
The system wants to see
another black family
going back and forth
to the court.
Life's a game of inches—
I refuse to fall short.
Daddy duties
I always give my portion
A man who neglects his kid
is committing a non-violent abortion
As a man
no matter what
you have to set the tone.
Think about that,
if you're young and want to be grown;
I'd be lying if I said
 it doesn't hurt
doing this
alone.

All Cried Out

I'm all cried out
I ran out of tears
Love, Pain, and Glory
Was a gift to share,
Reflection of my life
Journey through the years
I stayed in my own lane
But surpassed many peers,
Devil called and God picked up
I wasn't even there
Letting God and my family down
honestly was my biggest fear.

Broken Heart

Don't hate the player,
hate the game
Heartbreak is why they're not the same.
They fell deep
for the deceit
Heart sold for cheap with no receipt,
Everyone and everything has a secret
Some relationships function
Indiscreet.
Is it human nature to cheat?
We all know cheating is a sin
but is the urge to do so—
is it naturally instilled in all women
and men?
What will a dog or any other animal do?
We should all honestly think
these questions through.
If we really knew the true facts,
we'd probably all be single
and that's not what we want to do.
Everyone has been scorned
and had their hearts torn
Don't be upset
when they play hard to get
It's a 50/50 chance they may be legit,
But the other half reveals itself
during a tough situation
You can always see in the beginning
if the relationship will last forever
or end in a separation.
We all come with baggage
filled with insecurities and trust issues
Would you be willing to help go through it
and be ready to
hold them tight with tissues?
Understand that everyone has a past
Where they were once vulnerable
and moved fast
Understand when an argument
or disagreement occurs
It's nothing but drama
stemmed from built-in trauma.

Protection

My mouth is my gun
and my words are my bullets,
You will feel every shot
When I pull it.
God is my bullet proof vest
I'm always on safety,
Even when I rest
I'm always 7-fold,
I always keep words in the chamber
So quick to reload,
Can't run out ammo
Get a grip
Too much to handle,
Going all out with my words
Just like I'm Rambo.

Cheers to Success

Made it out the dirt
now we here
Bottles in the air
as we cheer
We pour a little out
for the ones who aren't here.
Eyes on the prize—
the finish line is near
It sounds crazy but success
is something that some people fear
Because on that journey
you're bound to lose some things
But you will also gain
and maintain some things,
Despite the Love and the Pain
It's all growth that the Glory brings,
To overcome any struggle is a blessing
After all the anxiety and stressing
You deserve all the greatness the world has to offer
When it comes to your life
You're your own author
Put your heart into it like when you cook,
It's all going to come together
and next thing you know
you have your own book.

Hard Part of Life

The hardest part of life
is when you have to let go,
When the time run out
no matter what
you have no say so.
Be grateful for the moments
because they leave a lasting memory,
I know the pain and hurt—
you invested so much energy.
But life moves on
so, you have to adapt,
The marathon continues
just keep running every lap,
They say time heals all wounds
and that's a fact,
But we just can't assume.
If it's really meant for you
then it will come back
and you shall decide
if you'd like
to resume.

Eye Opener

Black man on a mission
trying to save the youth.
If you're not educated,
then you probably won't fully
understand the truth.
I'm trying to open eyes.
It's like some are blind
or have a stye.
You can't ride the fence forever
so, you'll eventually
have to pick a side.
Take a mental day off work
You're going to need a bye.
Get prepared for the playoffs
and treat it like a layoff.
Narcissistic tendencies
called that "Hitler,"
so, watch out and understand
who you Ate off (Adolf)
I know it's kind of deep
but I hope you get it.
You won't understand it fully
until you really live it.

Please, Think!

Growing up
you have to learn to take baby steps.
Pay attention of what's in front of you
and forget what's next.
Try not to stress,
even if you get a crazy text.
Always stay strapped up
for that wild and crazy sex.
Stack your money and invest
Try not to fall in debt.
Life's a gamble
Just make sure you place your bet.
Things going to come at you fast
Just be prepared for it,
Deleted memories
Got people trying to restore it.
They trying to take you back
Lost and found in the streets,
Got you on your back
That's why it's called the "Trap"
Bars went over your head.
I hope you think of that.

Thanksgiving

Every day for me is THANKSGIVING
so that's why I always give THANKS
and remain GIVNG.
I celebrate alone when I do good deeds.
When it comes to P.R.E.V.A.I.L,
I make sure I water and nurture all seeds.
God giving gift in the present
Is to foresee.
This apple right here fell far from the tree
The Libra in me won't let me take a side,
I live this holiday everyday with no day off
So prepare your food for thought
if you're down to ride.
I'm in the middle with the saying that,
"numbers don't lie,"
The best part of THANKSGIVING
Is the humble pie,
My first conscious experience
was my time to arrive.
Last Supper will be my time
with my loved ones who truly believed
as we celebrate with a feast
When we think things are going wrong,
our moral compasses point east.
Happy THANKSGIVING
don't sound like a murder to me,
But I do understand the history
and why it was stated on the verse for "Free."
I have my own meaning but
I'm no jive turkey.
But I am who God want me to be.
Glory to God why I'm still living
And blessed to P.R.E.V.A.I.L
and be in position to still be giving.
When we all are Happy
then we make it
THANKSGIVING!

Break the Cycle

I sold weed but I could never sell cane
I saw what it did to my family—
Probably drove a few insane.
Out of respect, I won't even say any names.
I don't come around often,
they probably think I'm strange.
I'm just trying to break cycles
While I'm in my own lane.
I was named after 3 kinfolks
But made my own name.
My uncle got mad at me
Because I said we're not the same.
When he looked in my eyes
I know I sparked his brains.
Reminiscing from the past
I know it brought some pain.
I shook him up with my words
so I know I hit a nerve.
Stand for something or fall for anything.
Life is all free will
Don't be a "puppet on a string"
I'm speaking to you from the heart.
You're a king or queen.
Time to grow up now
and can't be stuck
like you're still in the teens.
Reality lies
but make sure you trust in your dreams!

Believe in Me

Like my momma would say,
"You going to miss me when I'm gone,"
I know I always think I'm right
I'm sorry if I'm ever wrong.
I apologize and it's coming from the heart.
I'll do it all over, just tell me where to start?
I'm being real, no time for being smart.
Tell me what you want? tell me what you need?
I'm praying to God
while I'm on my hands and knees
I can't bail out but I'm willing to plea,
Only tattoos, no tricks up my sleeves,
I understand we all need time to grieve
But please take time to believe....
Please Believe
in Me!

11:11

11:11 is a spiritually divine time.
Strength from positive energy
to leave the past behind.
Connection with God and the universe.
Blessings coming your way
and eliminating any type of curse.
God and the universe
work in mysterious ways.
Supreme Understanding
when you see that time on
random days.
Don't force it
and just know that it will come to you.
Just pay close attention to every clue.
11:11 pop up,
don't just make a wish
but speak all of your goals
and desires into existence.
Because God and the universe
will always give
Assistance.
11:11 is the date I chose to give
Love, Pain, and Glory:
The Last Tears.
2020 was tragic
but was the most spiritually awakening
time in many years.
Time to release all negative energy
and make amends to many of your fears.
We all had the devil on one shoulder
and the Angel on the other shoulder
metaphorically whispering in our ears.
Brush that evil shoulder off,
that's what they mean
when they say,
"the devil got kicked out of Heaven."
Remain spiritually connected
and acknowledge the time
when you truly see
ELEVEN, ELEVEN.

Love My Siblings

4 brothers and 1 sister.
We've been through so much
God was really with us.
We could have been dead
or lost to the streets,
I guess those whippings paid off
before we went to sleep.
Some will call it abuse
They are thinking too deep.
It was all discipline \
even with times on punishment
That kept us all in line.
Now-a-days it's like the kids are in control
As they know and can manipulate the system
Forcing others to be quick to dial
which leave them waiting on line.
Growing up we shared some great memories.
Siblings forever.
Our times together
Could have been a little better.
But we made the best of it.
Mom and Pops stuck it out for us
They could have gotten a divorce
and said, "enough of this!"
Can't forget the times we played video games,
cracking jokes, playing tag,
and more but it's too much to name.
Us spending quality time together
kept us all sane.
To be honest,
tomorrow is never promised.
We were all raised to win.
Let's please come together
once again
as siblings and take a family portrait.
As the youngest,
I don't mind telling all
I just pray you all agree
and support this.

The View

You can talk all day until your face is blue,
People still can't see it even with the clues.
They may be convinced if they watch the news,
But they fail to realize, it's coming from one view.
Anything you want to learn you can go on YouTube.
Just remember don't abuse it as your first go to.
Technology can help or hurt, it's a powerful tool.
Be wise and don't allow it to make you out to be a fool.

The Awakening

I woke up and I rose from the concrete.
If you understand me then your mind's deep.
Flashbacks from the devil to remind me.
I called God and was told "keep going"
Everywhere I go I be tiptoeing.
I don't step on toes
That's not how I roll,
I'm from a city where it's dark and cold.
The wrong mistakes could make you fold.
I stand up for what I believe in
and keep my feet on the ground.
Keep your head up and never put it down.
Know your purpose and uplift those in your town.
Have to keep our youth off the streets.
Have to teach safe sex
before they hit the sheets,
Have to raise our youth
To be Kings and Queens.
Paved the way for them
so they can fulfill their dreams.
We could make anything come true
as long as we
work together as a team.

Follow My Path

I woke up from my dream
so deep I really seen it.
Conscious thoughts to help change the world
Rem sleep—I really dreamed it.
Divine messages come to mind
It's the perfect time,
We're isolated in quarantine
God given sign,
Don't get stuck in the past
We can't rewind the time,
Embrace the everyday struggle
even if the sun don't shine,
Create a plan with some goals
to outshine your foes,
Stand on your words like your toes
and try not to fold,
Just follow my path,
I'll show you where to go.

7,7...

7, 7... I leave the last one for you
I hope *Love, Pain, and Glory*
helps lead you to your completion
and get you through.
Time of resurrection coming
And it already started in you.
Keep faith and follow
the divine sequence.
like the energy of frequency.
Numbers symbolize a lot so...
7s' spiritual symbol
is of the perfect world,
completion,
and Heaven.

Distant Lovers

It's like every woman in the world
is scorned.
I need an ultrasound to show proof
that you've
developed and grown,
and I want to be anxious to see
like when a baby is born.
I think about you queen
like a kid alone away from home
by himself in his dorm.
I need you close in distance to me
as you watch
and feel me perform.
Feel my poetic tongue as I go deep
without being asked.
I might mumble while I'm doing it.
It might feel
uncomfortable at first like we both
afraid of covid-19
so let's keep close to each other
but we're skin to skin
masked.
I want to make your body shiver
after I warm each
muscle in your body.
I need you to become my social
butterfly.
Let's create fireworks as we stand
together
like it's Juneteenth
with passionate love making with
4 play as
we gain each other's independence
like July.
Let's share each other's Love, Pain,
and Glory
to see if we're compatible or
equal.
I need your head into my head
As you feel my prequel and
sequel.
Take in my Last Tears
as you feel me cumming!
Don't run away once you see who
I'm becoming.
I need you to hold me down and
try different positions
and not be afraid to ride.
I need you to be my Bonnie as I'll
be your Clyde.
I want you to be my baby gyal
If not, can you please be my
romantic pen pal?
Let's write about love, social
issues, and random things
like chain letters for instance.
Can we discover true love through
our words long
distance?
I know you're probably afraid
like you're clinching tight
as if I'm trying to take your
pocketbook.
You could open it up and tease me
with your words as I look.
I hope you feel me go deep as I
touch your soul.
Pulling up to your spot 7 o'clock
on the dot like Nice
and Slow.
Penetrating while hitting your
inner G.
I want to uplift you to reach
climax through
our passionate love exchange of
energy.
Hug me tight while I'm inside
Let me know you got me like
scratches on my back as we say
together;
I'm cumming!........ but I have to
slide
Back to work but Distance Lovers
is your choice to
Decide.

Attention

I remember the day she told me she loved me
but I didn't believe it.
Actions speak louder than words
and I couldn't see it.
She was like most females still stuck on their ex.
I had to spend a lot of money
and give her good sex.
And when I gave all of that,
I was confused like: "what to give next?"
Over time I realized
it's more about giving attention.
Give lots of compliments and be spontaneous
Without having to mention.
For example, come home and tell them to get dressed.
Surprise them with something special
which is a great way to impress.
It will help spice up the relationship and relieve stress.
Understand there's always a need to fulfill
and if you don't do it,
best believe someone else will.

Thank You, Too!

I want to take the time to say, "thank you,
as you supported me through my breakthrough."
You know I'm talking to you.
If you're reading this,
Here's your special shout-out
so you know what it is.
I'll never forget you because
I heard what you said,
and I know what you did.
You're even more special
if I ever invited you to my crib.
I'm only one man, so I can't please everyone.
We're all on the run because it's a marathon.
We'll meet at the finish line if we won.
It will be like a track-meet when it's all said and done.
It's a lie if I said I did it without you.
No individual shout-out—I'll pout too.
Was going fishing mentally
and caught my trout men!
(Trotman!)
I can hear your voice calling me boo.
First name Charise
but more like She Rise.
Low and high-tide point of my life
forced me to go on a fishing trip
so, I found you during my internship.
True love and affection, no lie.
Thank you all who kept close to my neck
When I switched it up like a bow tie.
Thank you for believing in me
and giving me your time.
It's worth more than every penny
more like every dime.
You're never truly appreciated and respected
until you're gone.
At last, thanks to the doubters who added energy
To my light that turned me on.
Sometimes what's already been said before
don't need to be explained.
It was all written in our essence by God
so it's ordained.

Divorce or Lifetime of Happiness

It's a blessing the day your mom gave birth to you.
Free will so you can do what you want to do.
But I know grown people
who have a curfew.
Puppet on a string, more of a slave
and far from a queen or king
due to the power of a ring.
Things you've done in the beginning
probably won't be the same thing.
Probably asking yourself,
"why things really change?"
It might be too late
so that thought is way out of your range.
You're committed, so you're all in it.
They say it's cheaper to keep them
but that's when the money talks.
It isn't easy to just take the rings off
and take off on a permanent walk.
Question you should ask:
"Is this my best friend?"
If your answer is, "no"
Then it potentially might end.
This advice is for us all
who's already or planning to get married.
It's "Til death do us part"
With that being said,
He or She who marries his/her husband or wife:
Prepare for a divorce.
He or She who marries his/her best friend:
Prepare for a lifetime of happiness.

The Time

The time is here
so I'm willing to confess.
Was an alcoholic
at the time of a lot of stress.
Dad didn't know about it,
mom kind of knew
Everything was on a hush because of the struggle
we been through.
Everything was hand-me-downs,
hardly brand new
Wasn't special but I knew I was
apart of the chosen few.
Langston Hughes of my era.
Hip-Hop, to me, is the Blues.
Despite all of my struggles
I still pursue to pay my dues.
Try walking a mile or more
In my Payless Shoes.
I'm taking walks with no worries
stacking money like a Jew.
I overcame a lot in life
so I know
you can do it too.

Hug

Everybody needs a hug.
It's special on you like a ladybug.
The affection makes it feel real.
It's not the same as a handshake
because that makes it feel more like a deal.
Emotions grow from the feel.
It makes your eyes watery
 like an onion after a peel.
Give a hug and hold it tight.
Position can be determined by height.
Right one can uplift
someone's heart like a takeoff flight.
I know many don't like to hug
for whatever reason
but it's vitamin C for the body
so call it orange squeezing.
It's like wearing a mask
To protect you
but you feel it at that moment when it's hard to breathe.
The painful feeling
like when a baby teethes.
It's all love applied to growth
so open up and reach out
It always takes both.

Journey of Writer's Block

To still be alive, it's a
celebration!
Graduated from school,
congratulations!
You already beat the odds
because you paved the way.
Don't pay attention to the
critics and what they have to
say.
Everyone is entitled to their
own opinion.

(Keep grinding even when
others don't see!)

No matter what I go through
I'm always going to
P.R.E.V.A.I.L.
Quarantine had me locked
serving time inside a cell.
Bounce back on my feet
Flashbacks when I fell.
Stayed back in the first grade
Couldn't read nor spell.
Now my words on a different
level
giving people heaven and hell.
Painting vivid pictures
Call me Leo da Vinci.
Wake me up from this dream
Nerves shocked so try to pinch
me.

(Do You See It?!)

Thank you, baby-mama,
For not giving this Libra too
much drama.
Creativity on a different level
Call me the Black Futurama.
Crying out for help but they
not hearing me.
Ran out of tears now the whole
world could see.
Before I leave the world,
I left my legacy.
I manifest P.R.E.V.A.I.L as
my destiny.

(She helped put this together!)

We may flock together
but the black sheep gone
astray.
Lost on the road
already looked both ways.
Watch out for the signs;
It's easy to go the wrong way.
Everybody could preach
but who could make you stay?
They can keep you in prayer
But do they really pray?

(We still here!)

Before it's game time
prepare with a walk through.
Real-life situations
so plan for what you need to
do.
Punctuality with appropriate
apparel is important as
first impression
and don't forget to be prompt
too.

(Look good, feel good, do
good!)

Grew my hair out plus I have
tattoos.
That alone is a stigma as I'm
compared to other
criminals.

Some people don't listen, so
I'll continue to stay low key
and shoot subliminals.

(Be yourself no matter what
happens!)

Growing up we had to deal
with family dysfunction.
Main focus was immediate
family, so we barely had a
family function.
I do recall attending one
family reunion.
It usually takes death or
tragedy for a family to become
a union.

(The truth always hurt!)

Someone tried to wet me up
and catch me slipping in
the matrix but I stood up.
Don't matter how many times
you get knocked down
but it's how you bounce back
up.
To this day I still believe she
tried to set me up.
Another dude tried to crack me
out
but I slid through the crack
while God had my back and
got me out.
You have a lot of hurt people
who want to turn others out.
Kill them with success by
displaying your resilience
and how you turned out.
Plenty of deep lines to lift you
high once you figure
them out.
But most of my dope lines are
self- explanatory to
what I'm truly about.

(Life is full of different levels
and stages!)

I was up late packing bags.
Look under my eyes, tell me if
it's bad.
Kept a normal face but inside
was feeling sad.
The day I became a man I had
to salute my dad.
Everything we see, has a price
tag.
I'm so humble that it's hard for
me to brag.
I don't need a lift; I'll refuse a
cab.
Most things controlled
Was first performed in a lab.
Everybody was good
Until something turned them
bad.

(Don't worry too much about
how you've started but how
You'll finish!)

Sometimes you have to take
the pain and turn it to
passion.
Be humble as you remain in a
professional fashion.
Some people just want to
knock you off because
you're on.
For no reason just to turn your
lights out.
They chose to go the wrong
route in life so the
jealousy and envy come
because you chose to go the
right route.

(Life is based on free will, so
you choose what you
really want!)

This unfinished business is
what I was writing about.
I lost my train of thought
consciously not knowing it
was a fixed amount.
The plan was to shed my Last
Tears once I reached 77.
I wanted to take you on a
Journey of Writer's Block.
So on one cruise trip I gave
you a total of eleven.
I reminded all my love ones
that the release date will
be 11/11.
I know someone
mathematically inclined
will say but you gave us a total
of 88.
Just know I spoke things in 2
existence.
You and me on this journey of
2,
I pray we somehow connect
and relate.
I tried to give everyone a piece
making sure they ate.
88 plus 2 is 90.
The year I was born to be our
leader.
My time is now, and I ask you
nicely to stand up and
stand beside me and be more
than just a reader.

(P.R.E.V.A.I.L is a journey
you must be willing to take as
you plant your seeds and
watch it grow!)

Born Genius

Flashback came to mind
back when I was young.
Stayed back in the first grade,
I swear I felt dumb
Been going through the struggle
That's why my feelings are numb.
I might not say a word but listen.
I might just put up a thumb.
I'm all about respect
while my mind is worth more than any check.
I'm a born genius check out what I plotted next.
I rather speak in person
instead of calling or sending a text.
I put my cards in hand in order.
I'm not worried about the deck.
I set myself free.
But still have a chain around my neck.
Just a reminder to never forget my roots.
Kunta Kinte drive—
had to take off the noose.
Can't keep this elephant chained,
I'll always get loose.
Feel my energy when I walk in a room.
Black Albert Einstein,
judge me by my mind and not by
the way that I'm groomed.
Always had my eyes on the stars.
Never been afraid to shoot
 because at least if I fall
short I'll land on the moon.
Mamba mentality so I took multiple shots.
Leader of this generation
I knew there would be vacant spots.
The way I think is different like another planet.
I've started to believe that I'm an anointed seed
That God planted.

YES, I WILL!

True issues all because of what I've been through.
I apologize if you felt like I was against you.
I realize that it's all in my mental.
Unfinished business got me sentimental.
I just want the chance to love again.
Here, take my heart let's start the bargaining.
Despite all the pain I just want to talk love.
I'll give you the world and go up and above.
I'm all about TLC so I'm far from a scrub.
I'll hold your body close & tight like a bear hug.
Pac definition so know you're dealing with a THUG.
Let's help build each other up and make sure
each other's good.
I'm going deep in you like I'm heading back to the hood.
We all have some type of Krazy side.
Just hold my hand and let me know
that you're down to ride.
I've grown up as a man so judge what's inside.
I'm here to pick you up because I know you fell.
You're probably thinking to yourself like:
"damn he knows me well"
You've pushed me away so many times
but I'm here still.
I know the day will come when you say,
"YES, I WILL!"

The Ghetto

Where I come from is called, "the ghetto"
also known as the inner-city slums.
We lack a lot of resources
so we scramble for crumbs.
Dog eat dog world so only the strong survives.
Kill or be killed is a game in the streets
to see who could stay alive.
Can't forget about the weak because
they also survive.
No matter if you're strong or weak,
everybody could still persevere.
Look around and you can see a lot of resilient people
still here.
Ghetto lifestyle left us scarred.
Raised in a disadvantage in which we have to work
twice as hard.
A dog is a man's best friend.
Some turn snake at the end
and bites the hand that feeds them.
Eyes and mouth wide open as they turn to Venom.
Segregation played a major role in why almost every
city has a ghetto.
Our voices are ignored when we cry for help
so that's why we resort to violence
because it has more of an effective echo.
They do say, "actions speak louder than words"
so that's why we express our frustration and aggression
with verbs.
Government assistance come in hand
especially when we live in a capitalist country
that thrives off supply and demand.
Families should also not abuse the system
and just live off people's hard earned tax dollars
in which I truly understand.
Powder milk I couldn't stand
but the peanut butter and government cheese
made some amazing cookies and grilled cheeses
To truly understand the ghetto, you have to live in it.
That's why I use my words
to help give those who don't know a glimpse of it.
Most importantly to see where myself
and my people come from
and reasons why we tend to march
to the beat of our own drums.

Being Black

Being Black in AmeriKKKa
we have to stand tall
Is being Black
really scaring you all?
Why does Blackness
have you so intimidated?
Is it the thought of mixing Black
and white together
which could force the white race
to be eliminated?
We all in this together,
I thought the country was a
melting pot?
Since slavery, there were laws
and doctrines to stop
blacks with a strategic plot.
If you need proof go check out the
Willie Lynch letter.
Ways to make a slave and also
have Blacks go against
each other to see who's better.
Think about it
after you read it and ask yourself
is it still relevant?
Some of our people still suffer
from a syndrome called
the "chained elephant"
Being Black comes with natural
power
Balled fist in the air don't be a
coward
We needed leverage for justice, so
it didn't hurt to bust
a Knee Kap!
It woke the world up and exposed
the true K's in
AmeriKKKa.
Time to create a New World in
America.
Being Black is a struggle but it's
also a Blessing.
We need to teach more Black
History in schools
and I promise our kids will be
engaged no matter the lesson.
Being Black is a gift to the world.
Even with our hands up they don't
acknowledge that
we're present.
Being Black has it's pros and
cons.
Being Black in power,
they don't want you to respond,
They are hoping that money talks
and it will keep your
mouth shut.
And if you don't oblige,
you become a sacrificial lamb.
I don't know if it's true,
but I heard they gave us the Bible
in exchange for the land.
Please don't quote me on that and
don't get too emotional.
I'm just speaking about Being
Black in AmeriKKKa
and getting people to think without
taking things so personal.
Being Black in all forms is a rarity
despite any disparity.
Red, white, and blue are the colors
that we're used to from the flag to
the flashing lights.
Get prepared and learn your rights.
True colors come out when they
give US a black and blue.
Being Black and speaking the
truth get US scrutinized.
Our 3rd-eye woke up and now we
realize.
Being Black is everything and it's
written.
Only one original down to every
invention.
The red blood on the leaves, you
have to see it in order to believe.
After reading "Being Black," it
might change how you act.
When you think all of this
through,
please close your eyes
while you envision and feel
every whip on your back.
That's how it feels Being Black.

The Key

I wake up late nights
with a lot on my mind.
I understand the saying
"Just take one day at a time."
New Year's resolution
With a lot in store.
No Scarface
But guarantee the World Is Yours.
Staying patience is the Master key
to open up many doors.
You're the Locksmith of your life
so open it up.
Despite any struggle,
you were built to be tough.
Just shake off the rust and
believe In God We Trust.

Driven

-With Judy Denny

(Judy Denny)
I have to stay driven
When what I worked hard for is not given,
The pigment of my skin
Does not reveal the gifts I have within.

I am put in a box
They need me to stop,
They don't want a black woman to lead,
They want to continue to
deceive all.

They don't want me to rise
For I will take them by surprise,
For what they tried to hide
Continued to grow and thrive.

They say Black Lives Matter to us,
But there are no black executives they trust,
To be at the table and make decisions,
I am just a number, and not part of the visions.

I am a modern-day slave who serves,
But not advanced to where I deserve.
They want me to stay in my place,
Because the truth, they don't want to escape.

It hurts that I am more than qualified,
But because I don't look like them, my promotion is not justified.
No matter how much they try to stop me,
I have to stay driven and succeed,

(Leo James)
Hands on the wheel I have to stay driven,
Foot on the pedal knowing success is never given,
We strive to beat the odds on our pursuit of happiness
for a better living.

Intelligent black man gets overlooked,
They act surprise when they see you reading a book,
They ask a lot of questions because the
Neurotransmitters released through the synapse which
have them intrigued or shook.

Many forces are deep when you study the mind,
I dumb myself down at times just to think about the
time when I was left behind,
I'll drive someone to the limit
Treat them like a foreign car that's one-of-a-kind,
Get them noticed knowing I'll get pulled over and fined,

Speeding in the fast lane, I know when to slow it down,
I always observe and notice who's around,
Perfectionist, I don't mind going back around,
You always see things different the second time around.

I keep going and stay driven like a 24/7 machine,
The hood in me pop up and I run to the scene,
I can see myself now in a visible meme.

I drove my Kat Kat to use her poetic tongue,
The dog came out of her as she spitting pain like blood
from her heart to her lungs

Dramatic Reading Contest was our first performance
and Driven is our first gospel song

You gave me six hugs(stanzas) so it's only right I give
you seven hugs(stanzas)
No competing but completion together to P.R.E.V.A.I.L
Sorry to bring this up but you were a Valedictorian
Native daughter of the city but was rejected from Yale
But that just kept you driven
Eye to eye they just couldn't see your vision

I won't say much more but this piece of art together is
an example of rehabilitation
Breaking our family cycle is a celebration
I love you and keep driven, we remain first
Our words together about to make someone going the
wrong way reverse
Dramatic Reading 2 during one of my motivational
speeches will be real and not rehearsed.

US VS. THEM

Once one's eyes fully open, they will see the truth
which will seem crazy.
We have to educate our kids, no time to be lazy.
They're trying to stop our future so they're starting with
our babies.
It's the same way when crack hit back in the 80's.
The New Jim Crow also known as Mass Incarceration.
Daddy locked up, not around to help with maturation.
Now our youth are being raised in the same system.
"We're guilty until proven innocent."
So how can we really convince THEM?
It's like all odds against US to put the majority of US behind the wall.
We in it like crabs in a bucket.as they're watching hoping we fall.
We have to show them we can make it out without having to just rap or
ball.
They're aiming for US like a hole in one, they out here
playing golf.
Make it to the top, it's either THEM or our own trying to
knock US off.
Prime example, do your research and look up Malcom X
Pray every day that none of US are next.

Real Talk

Do Not Enter: I know you probably don't see the sign.
The streets are a trap that was purposely well design
If you decide to go that route, please proceed with caution
Let me talk to you even if you heard these things often
I just want to keep you from sleeping in a cell or an expensive coffin
Please think, because you can always go a different path
I understand school can be boring because it's more than just simple math
Other option is that you can pick up a trade and learn a skill
Not much of a loan like school but more like a hefty bill
It won't take your whole life to pay it off
It's a sacrifice for a better gain
Don't look at it as taking a loss
It's a smart way to be self-employed
And be your own boss
You'll be building your own team to
Coach in your own field
It will be a positive hustle
Without having worries of getting arrested or killed

Black Sheep from the Herd

I downplayed my intelligence.
Why'd I do that?
Just to stay cool and relevant.
Main focus in the room
I was the elephant.
But one day I got caught
from my 6th-grade teacher.
He scouted me like a coach
analyzing from the bleachers.
He took me from my hood class
to his upper class
I just wanted to goof off
and show my ass.
It taught me that friends come and go
but lessons last.
Black sheep roaming around with the herd.
Shoutout and salute to Mr. Hurd
and all the troopers at Troup.
We took all the outer-city educators
to our inner-city stoop.
But only a chosen few could relate.
Culture shock is a feeling that you either love or hate.
It's always someone that see potential in you that you
can't see.
I still remember him giving me that "D" on my report card
and to this day I disagree.
So disappointed that summer that I couldn't be me.
It added fuel to my fire.
It's part of the main reason
why my desire is to inspire.
Oregon Trial assignment,
I still remember the script.
It's a reason I do a lot of foreshadowing
In every piece of manuscript.
Like "Man's Search for Meaning"
I can relate during 2020 quarantining.
It introduced me to creative writing.
Love, Pain, and Glory: The Last Tears is my journey
from beginning to end of
some of my deepest pieces from highlighting.

Son of an Undertaker

They say no question is dumb
So, don't be afraid to ask it.
Used to visit the funeral home
Put my hands all in the casket.
I was young and fascinated with death.
Count your blessings every day.
Never know when you'll take your last breath.
My dad is the Undertaker, I'm not talking wrestling.
People had to die in order for us to eat.
Sound crazy but that was our financial blessing.
We used to greet our dad and ask him
 how many bodies he got?
It was all a part of the business
and if you weren't familiar then it will seem weird
to overhear that conversation on the spot.
My grandmother used to say he was happy when people died
but when they didn't, he was not.
Dealing with death he was always on call.
When it comes to dead bodies, he's seen it all.
So death to me has always been normal
like when I communicate it's informal.
He's the main reason I'm a giver and not a taker,
You can't take nothing with you when you die and
money comes and go
are the words to the son from an undertaker.

Hood Poet

I remember I used to struggle as a reader but writing
came naturally to me.
Painting vivid imagery with my words while creating art through
literature for the world to
cherish and see.
Hood poet in the flesh but failed to realize it at first.
I wrote all my scriptures and testimonies
and like I mentioned before,
I've been an example through my
last tears as how the last become first.
All the jewels I've been giving out is pure, so you know
it's real.
Food for thought so I prepped a Thanksgiving meal.
Please enjoy it but I hope we all can agree that it's
a good steal but let it all resonate before moving
impulsively like a Black Friday deal.
Look deep into my eyes and see the red shot of blood.
Use your 3rd eye and split the image to truly
understand the flood.
That's how you determine which side to pick.
Remember to keep your head down and follow through
while all eyes will be on you,
from All-Area and All-State
just to see how you kick.
Was forgotten many times but one time was placed at
the host/head of the table.
From a special team to help keep the offense and
defense as a whole stable.
Every point connects that's why it becomes seven after
the six.
It's now time to pick a side like practice so you get
caught in the mix.
Always played the field whether it was a classroom,
in the streets, or an actual field.
Always been a team player and ready to build.
Only get one shot while others get several.
Only a chosen few truly understand once they
reach a higher level.

Unify

When we stand as one then
that's the moment we unite.
Peaceful protest is a
positive way to shed light.
Fist in the air
so no physical fight.
Change gone come just
don't expect it overnight.
Everybody in the world
have to play his/her part.
Detox any hatred that's
imbedded in the heart.
We all in the same race
While some just had a head start.
Everything that's controlled has its own theory.
Patiently awaiting change for years just made us weary.
Mistreated when we all should have been treated equal.
Police brutality, racism, poor education system, mass
incarceration, and others was all designed to be unequal.
The whole world sees what's going on.
Revolution happening because it's been too long.
Give us reparation, justice, and equity while
admitting what was done for years was wrong.

Venting

Throwback moment—
Not only on a Thursday.
Looking for flaws
then catch me on an off day.
Sleeping on me
I promise I'll make you all pay.
I was gaining knowledge
while some was playing in the hallways.
I was stacking money
while some was coping all the J's.
"He thinks he's better then everyone."
Guess what? that's what they all say.
I've never really cared
because I knew who I was.
Real recognize real
was tainted in my blood,
You have to go through the pain
just to understand the love.
I could keep on going
But I vented and that's enough.

The Voice

I'm speaking to the youth like I'm speaking to the choir.
I pray that my words spread like a wildfire.
When they see it, I know they're going to spread the word.
Working on my proposal, I believe I'll be heard.
I'm putting pressure until the city officials let me in.
We P.R.E.V.A.I.L so it's only right that we win.
My voice God gave me is so powerful.
Inner-city kid who listen that's why I'm knowledgeable.
Soaked in so much wisdom from all my elders.
I couldn't sit back and dwell knowing that the system failed us.
Everything strategic to put me in position.
It's a sacrifice hoping that my people listen.

Remember

I remember those days when I used to cry a lot.
I always stayed humble so I could earn my spot.
I was taught to work hard until my body stop.
People hit me like a pinata just to see me pop.
Passive-aggressive like I'm feeling restless.
"I can't breathe," they leave our brothers breathless.
"Black Lives Matter" I hope the world get the message.
I remember History because it's His Story.
Rose Grew from Concrete that's what you call glory.
Remember that today is a Mystery.
Tell yourself every day that it's "My Story"
Keep your story organized like an inventory.
Remember to share it out and don't keep it bottled in.
Seek out your purpose from your heart it's all within.
God won't leave nor forsake you despite your sin.
Remember to count your Blessings and be grateful.
Just remember that some will love and hate you.
But it's someone out there that can relate to you.
Most importantly, remember how far you've come.
It's a marathon so you're far from done.

Parenthood

Credit score getting closer to my kid bedtime.
For those who don't hit me up just know I'm fine.
I've been doing this alone for so long now.
Rose grew from the concrete
it's hard to tell you how.
Being single and raising a kid is not easy
I'll tell you that.
I salute all the single parents
so I tip my cap.
I salute all the co-parents
despite being separated they still have the kid(s) back.
Working together could dictate how the kid[s) act.
I take pride in being the greatest parent despite
personal issues, I've always tried to be transparent.
Keep raising your kid(s) to achieve great things.
They will be our next leaders amongst our other
queens and kings who will all stand together as one.
Reciting the words from speeches, poems, and songs
about change and the things, we've all done.

Unfinished Business

Have you ever had the Devil come knock at your door?
You don't have time for drama, so you choose to ignore.
Still remember the guilty pleasure
due to being bored.
Playing different games with meanings
moving around the board.
Guess what? That's the same as life.
They say iron sharpen iron but don't get stabbed with a
knife.
That's called betrayal, I know it happened to you before.
It'll take you back down memory lane like a line at a Black Friday door.
Our brains document traumatic events.
It's like the memory automatic record.
That's why it's hard to go away.
Unfinished business that's what Gestalt will say.
We need true therapy not no medicated scheme.
Spy gate so I'm pulling plays from the other team.
Pardon my interruption of the cash cow.
I'm trying to open 3rd eyes so my people aren't shocked
at the end of the day like WOW!
Mental health is real but to misdiagnose someone
just to get paid is wild.
This only leads to creating an institutionalized child
who will then become an institutionalized adult.
Lack of effective therapy leads to that negative stigma
as the end result.
I saw it firsthand so I know the system could be foul.
Don't get confused like why foul don't rhyme with soul.
Keep doing your research and eventually you will know.
Some of the greatest stories are never told.
All prayers and calls will be answered.
Can't forever be declined or on hold.

Backwards

We're used to living backwards.
We force HIStory to repeat itself.
We want people and things we don't need.
We need people and things we don't want.
It's like we always want the good but settle for the bad.
Then we start to complain
We start with a smile but end with tears.
We tend to forget who was really there.
Through it all, we always seem to think back to recognize the ones who truly cared afterwards.

Pick Up the Pieces

Speak from the heart like a drunk mind speaking a
sober thought.
We all have past trauma
and several fights we fought.
We've been broken down so we're still picking up the
pieces.
P.R.E.V.A.I.L with Love, Pain, and Glory
without even knowing was already my thesis.
One piece after another can lead to purpose.
Don't get caught up in entertaining clowns because
you will become a part of the circus.
I live in a glass house, so I try not to throw rocks but I
know some people who threw rocks at my house.
I can't get distracted from a woman wearing a red
Blouse
or let a Benedict Arnold get close to my home.
Don't be surprised if your own family leaves you Home
Alone.
Just be prepared for whatever happens in life just in case you have to
pick up the pieces alone.

The Struggle

I kept it real, I wrote it down.
I had to publish it.
I did it on purpose, so people know that I'm legit.
Unfinished business is the past, so I had to dead it.
I' was trying to raise my kid and build up my credit.
I did it all alone but imagine if I had some help.
I needed motivation, so I grabbed a book straight from the shelf.
I always think about others
Before I think of self.
That could be an issue
Especially if I always do it.
I was raised to be a giver, so I'm used to it.
I could be misunderstood that's why I love music.
The struggle taught me a lot, same time it made me hood.
It taught me how to be resourceful so I'm forever good.

What? Keep!

What you do when you want something?
Keep going!
What if they keep rejecting you?
Keep showing!
What if they're not hearing you?
Keep talking!
What if they knock you down?
Keep walking!
What if they take your light away?
Keep glowing!
What if life gets hard?
Keep living!
What if they're being selfish?
Keep giving!
What if they don't believe your story?
Keep telling!
What if?.......
Keep Prevailing!

4 Me 2 You (Dedicated to Class of "09")

And in loving memory of Ja'na

No High School reunion
but you all know what I'm doing.
I'm proud of you all,
keep achieving all your goals
and don't stop pursuing.
No matter if your hand
was dealt badly
Just remember your life
is far from being ruined.
We know life's not even
so we have to beat the odds.
We can't look for no handouts.
We need to create our own jobs.
We know life's been a struggle.
My words are a stimulus check
They try to get to your head
so they aim for your neck.
Better stop playing checkers
and learn how to play chess.
Life is full of chaos
Just navigate through the mess.
Think about positive things
to avoid any stress.
If you're still breathing or reading this,
Thank God because you're Blessed.

Memory Lane

Flashbacks of when I used to be broke
from a snotty nose trying to sneak and smoke.
Took my mom's cigarette I lit it then I put it out.
Restraining order on my dad, he couldn't be around the house.
Mom had her best friend over-sleeping on the couch.
She used to slurp corn starch from a straw inside her mouth.
Talking daddy issues is the same feeling
I know about.
My sister and I had to visit him at the rooming house.
That same house my granddad owned and then sold it to my dad.
Talking about a bounce back.
Not everyone can do that which is sad.
He could have left for good and been a dead-beat dad but he didn't so I'm glad.
I understand the importance of having a father figure.
I've learned a lot as I've grown and gotten bigger.
I could have been aiming for the stars by pulling a trigger.
But instead I was saved by the moon.
When I could have been doomed.
It's a Blessing to be spiritually attuned.

Helping Hand

Writings on the wall but your back against the wall.
You fall and start losing things
like trees lose leaves in
the fall.
People see the paintings and writings
but might not understand the cry for help.
They act like they do or shrug and say, "welp
It's not my life so why should I care."
With no care in the world with a facial glare.
You'll find out that many people are selfish more than selfless.
They instantly forget about the times when they were helpless.
We all need help in order to be completely
self-sufficient.
We should all remember the struggle of learning basic skills and working towards being proficient.
To reach one is to teach one.
Supporting someone is a good deed that should
always be done.

Another

Another momma cries
Another fish fries
Another senseless killing being televised
Another broken heart
Another war to start
Another lost soul
Another crossroad
Another hard time
Another unsolved crime
Another warning sign
Another story headline
Another traumatic event
Another dollar being spent
Another lost sister or brother
Another thing after another

Karma

What goes around comes back around.
It's connected to the lost and found.
The universe sees everything.
Be mindful of what you sling.
Love, Pain, and Glory
of what you put out is what Karma will always bring.
Between the cold and hot seasons
always comes the spring.
That's when growth and new beginnings start.
Fall is when colors change, and things fall apart.
And winter is when things get cold and die off.
Then it's Spring back up on deck with Karma to leadoff.
Learn the rules of the Universe in all.
It all connects like a diamond in baseball.
See it though like a 3rd eye.
Experience the illuminated art
of life like a roll of a die.
Several chances of possibilities.
Karma dictates and distributes
all the probabilities.
It comes down to decisions you make like
Good or evil.
It's like losing something or adding something
To get you closer to
God or Devil.
Karna comes in different types and has different laws
that can play a role in many of your flaws.
Karma always makes return visits
like the law of physics.
Please be mindful of the energy that you give out.
You'll learn sooner or later on what Karma is about.
Karma gambles off emotions as it picks a random card.
Karma gives its all to the universe because it loves
hard.

F.O.E. (Family Over Everything)

I got my eyes on that cake
I want the Sugar slice.
Pound cake, pecans, with vanilla ice-"ing"
Name after my grandpa's
cause we kings.
They both are Free Masons.
They know and seen everything.
I thank my Aunt
She the reason that I'm here.
Don't hurt my cousins
I meant that Krystal, Clear.
Family over everything.
That's my first team.
Nothing comes in between
Not even the green.
I'm talking money
For those that don't understand.
No WILL or life insurance
But praying for a plan.
Give a helping hand.
Not saying free
but we have to avoid
cutting down our family trees.
Just like our love
our roots run deep.
I let the truth be told
So, it's no mystery
Let's all come together
and explore our family history.

Social Truth

I'm a leader in life I feel like I could save the day.
I understand like everything has a price to pay.
Just give me a chance so I could pave the way.
For my family, youth, and community.
Times like this you have to boost your immunity.
Since you opened up, this between you and me.
6 degrees of separation; that's how it be.
Social distance separation is 6 feet.
The distance from life and death is 6 feet.
Judgement day come, what's the distance for when we meet?
Social isolation: look it up. It's real deep.
It's going to all make sense when you peep game.
That's the truth when they say things won't be the same.
They say the truth hurts but lies kill.
No matter what keep faith and have hope still.

Stress

Try not to stress out because
they say it causes cancer.
You need prayer and support
It's believed to be the answers.
Forgive and forget
sound like a great mix.
You can't control everything
You might end up sick.
We gamble with a lot
just make a smart pick.
Checking out early
That's not solving it.
Keep faith
just know it always gets better.
Prepare for all types of change
just like the weather.
I've been writing a lot
but no death letters.
Love, Pain, and Glory
as I leave my mark on the world
Like the ones who did before me.
Study life in depth
but remember not to stress.

Controlled

Once we leave the pen,
We come out lost
and spill our ink on the streets.
We go back
like a drug user who relapses.
We fly kites from the outside to the inside.
We are told what to do like animals in cages and soldiers at war.
Learning to speak in codes. Stories are usually kept secret and untold.
The mind of the individual is being manipulated, conditioned, and controlled.

Born-Leader

Nothing in this world could stop me
because I'm highly favored.
When it comes to my city,
I could be the savior.
All based off my passion
I might just run for mayor.
I'm not serious but I might take it into consideration.
I'm a firm believer that I'm a leader of my generation.
I feel the pressure, but it feels more like an obligation.
All the words I've ever said going to be in quotation.
Book after book get ready put them in rotation.
I can't stop but I'm working like a machine.
I'm at the top but I go deep like a submarine.
Everything I'm doing right now was all in my dream.
Nightmares—I remember every tear and every scream.
Sometimes life can be an illusion
It's not always what I seem.

Dirty Streets

There's no love in the streets,
to be honest,
if you ask me.
I know you curious about the life,
so you want to see.
No lifeguards on duty to save you
from the sharks in the sea.
Watch your back everywhere you go,
You got some who like to creep.
Professional babysitters who'll rock you to sleep.
Barely say a word but might smile while they speak.
Mission on repeat while their endorphin levels increase.
Watch who you hang with
because some are street famous.
While you're in pursuit to get a name,
you might just end
up nameless.

P.R.E.V.A.I.L Part 3

Let me know what you want to do.
I don't mind walking you through every poem.
Trust me when I tell you, I know your mind is going to roam.
Call that a writer's and reader's vacation.
I take you back so you can feel some history like what
the Christians did to the Romans as clarification.
If you already know then you're with me.
We were all once blind until we had an awakening
experience that allowed us to truly see.
Please analyze every word and every line.
I'm hoping to bring my people to a deeper level of
consciousness like the meaning of mine.
George Bush came with the act called "No Child Left
Behind"
I was left behind because I was behind academically
which resulted due to my behavioral act, but I turned out fine.
I just needed a mentor and an extracurricular outlet.
So Mr. George and soccer are what God blessed me and allow me to
get.
They both taught me dedication and to never quit.
Appreciate and cherish my image when I wear my
chain, P.R.E.V.A.I.L shirt and blazer outfit.
Born to be an iconic figure for our youth.
I don't want to be a Martyr but whatever happens
happens as long as I fulfilled God's purpose and
delivered the truth.
We only leave moments and memories.
We only leave a kid(s) and a legacy.
I don't want to be taken out by any type of supremacy or jealousy.
I'm still here to smell so please give me every flower.
I'm going to tell you like I tell all my people
Stand up and say it loud,
"I P.R.E.V.A.I.L from At-Risk to
Empower!"

Paranoia

Been through a lot so enough is enough.
I've always believed in Blessings and not luck.
Sawed off shotgun coming at me
and being watched by a black truck.
Look around down and up—who to trust?
Think it's love but in disguise it's lust.
Trust issues but trying to give it a try.
Take things for face value with 3rd eye.
Feel like someone is looking for me
while I'm looking for myself.
Trauma from slavery to now.
Therapeutic exercises to enhance mental health.
Usage of words to describe feelings for the world to be felt.
Been came to realization of need for help
but pride and ego took control.
Warm heart-tempered turned cold.
Sign in front saying, "sold."
Going down an unexpected road.
Fixed praying hands forced to fold.
I pray the Lord my soul to take.
Forgive every sin and mistake.
Subconscious is wrong
while the conscious is right.
Internal affair fight
to seek the truth through hindsight.

Left on Read/Seen

Good heart reaching out
but was left on read.
No response so same feeling
as if someone is dead.
If the color's not green
They're not stopping for red.
I hope they hear me loud and clear
and everything I've said.
Don't be afraid of me
because I'm only human.
I know you've been hurt before but
I'm feeling the same too, damn.
Don't compare me to no other man.
Insecurity got you guarded so you won't understand
I WANT YOU!
But I'm not Uncle Sam.
Do you want a strong man?
Or do you want a young-minded man and hope to turn
him into a man?
If that's the case, sorry, I'm not it
but I wrote all my feelings out,
so I know you've seen it.

Praying Hands

Glory to God
hands together, so let us all pray.
Flashback being drunk driving the wrong way.
Tearing up the front of the car on and off the highway.
Yelling out TGIF: Thank God It's Friday
or even better yet it's Saturday.
It don't matter no more; it's just not the day.
No serious injuries or no cops around.
Don't believe in the most high? do you believe it now?
Plead the 5th or better yet just shoot it down
You have your own experience when you hit the ground.
Talking rock bottom or a dead end.
Your true purpose is usually found
With a verb carrying a "g" at its end.
Make it through the tunnel and you shall always see light.
Many of us are covered with the blood but your true
belief applies pressure to all wounds
 in which you'll feel it tight.
Religious but more spiritual.
Count your Blessings
and give a helping hand like a ritual.
Some believe in God and some believe in luck
Like the color green similar to an Irish clover filled with
symbolic meanings like a buck.
Hands together then we become ONE.
In God We Trust
with an illuminated eye to be awakened
and see what the power has done.

Pure Jewels

This might just be all words
but it's pure motivation.
Catch your dreams. Don't chase it.
No need for hesitation.
Always go with your gut feeling.
Aim for the stars, even if you don't,
At least aim for a ceiling.
We could all be heroes you don't have to be a villain.
Never wave the white flag
I don't care if that's your country.
Set goals daily, weekly, and monthly.
This will set you up for the year.
Remember not to live in doubt nor fear.
The world is yours,
I'm just giving you confirmation.
Every jewel being given
is just pure affirmation.

New Haven (Heaven)

New Haven is supposed to be a discovered place of safety.
No true community policing.
Like walk the beat and make sure some of our youth
make it home safely.
It's like there's a curse or dark cloud over the city.
It's like you have to throw a rock and be a bad boy like
HOV and Diddy.
Take time to understand me because my words can be witty.
Many men mindset like I'm 50.
You probably thinking age but I'm thinking cent.
We have to seek the guardian angels that's Heaven sent.
It's a divine experience of a new beginning.
When accomplishments symbolize winning.
First thought that come to mind of the city is Yale.
Pistol Waving New Haven is the name giving from the
streets that introduced our youth to hell,
that prepared them to self-destruct and go to jail.
When lessons aren't taught properly then that's why
our children fail.
When you're making positive moves
that's when the city
want to jump sail.
We will change the city's name and mindset
from New Haven to New
Heaven with P.R.E.V.A.I.L

Dreams to Reality

They say sleep is the cousin of death
But that's one cousin I haven't met yet.
I'm afraid to have dreams
because those dreams may become real
like a gunshot to the head
In my sleep I am dead, in reality I am alive
Dreams allow me to die
in order to wake up to reality.
Death sits on every corner
Like churches and liquor stores.
According to Freud, dreams are hidden
emotions and desires.
Dreams can get out of control
Like wildfires.
We decide to put them out or keep it going.
Pay close attention to every detail
because dreams be knowing.
We decide if we want to be
a dream catcher or a dream chaser.
Our thoughts manifest itself
through dreams like ink from a pen
In which we can't use an eraser.
It's already been permanently written.
Many books in history has been lost or rewritten.
The Love, Pain, and Glory series
will be one for the ages.
That will touch every reader's mind, heart, and soul
as they turn through the pages.

Greatness

First things first,
I'm in the kitchen because I like to cook.
Talking life recipes, I'm adding to the book.
Drawing pictures with my words tell me how it looks.
I'm a chef, I'm an artist—I can do it all!
If you need some motivation feel free to call.
Hold on tight and try not to drop the ball.
Ignore all the haters.
They're watching every move you make
because they're spectators.
Like the "Last Dance"
They're going to feel the greatness later
Keep doing what you do,
I'm so proud of you
Find your match.
get lit.
that's that added fuel.
Cruel world
but don't let it change
your attitude.

037

At times, it's like we're living backwards.
Turn your back and that's the time they recite words.
Take the time to see things from a different angle.
And if it's tied in a knot, you'll need patience to untangle.
When you finally find out, you're going to say O!
But now you know.
I'm a Libra, I was born October 3rd.
037 are just numbers but could it be a word?
3 family members have the same birthday
You probably thinking no way.
I was named after 3 relatives
Writing books was one of my greatest superlatives.
7 is the number of completion.
7th letter in the alphabet is a G.
Look it up and you shall see.
7 also represents P.R.E.V.A.I.L.
It's time to reveal how those special numbers can get you to spell.
Remember life is a thinking game.
Turn the title upside down
What's the name?

Speaking it in2 Existence

When I think of the number two.
Fell in love with only two.
Had two parents
Had two cars
Ran away from situations
I admit, I ran 2 far
Had two rings
Had two chains
Experience teach a lot
Which creates growing pains.
Had two bedrooms
Had two bathrooms
Tragic war event coming soon
It's about to be a 2nd baby boom
About to have two books published
About to have two shirt designs
Putting P.R.E.V.A.I.L in the forefront
I revealed it through many signs
About to have two houses
Maybe I might have two kids
Help put me in position 2 be our leader
I need every bid
About to have 2Pac/Machiavelli 's back
About to shine bright on stage in black
A Raisin in the Sun
Speaking things in 2 existence
Motivational speaking and writing books
Is my purpose which is 2 much fun.

Nirvana

If you really know me, then you can call me "Lee"
If you see my vision, then you can call me Spike Lee.
I've been patiently waiting so I'm "Doing the Right Thang"
I need my Nefertiti to believe in me and claim me as her king.
The love has to be deeper than the cost of a wedding and a ring.
The ladies I meet be so materialistic.
They don't be thinking about building for the future.
It's all about now far from being realistic.
I need her to rise and grind with me from sundown to sunup.
Not to leech off me for a come up.
Every date for me have to be food and Monopoly.
We could talk about love and owning some type of property.
We could talk about having a kid if the conversation deep and the vibe is right.
Then we can add a "S" to kid and close the book on our "EX"
Then we could come together and stimulate one another like "SEX"
I'm still living a Bachelor lifestyle until I Master it
I don't mind giving my heart, but I'm only giving half of it
When I finally decide to settle down, I'll have a Bachelor party with some Associates.
A moment to be flirtatious but appropriate.
Take me back to school, it'll be an honor to enroll in you
as you be my professor and tell me what I have to do.
Support one another to get through life like a semester and each trimester.
When I become a Master. I will achieve Nirvana and be called Dr. LOVE after.
Divine love where it feels like heaven.
Complete one another like the number 7.
See eye to eye like 11:11.

Mastermind

It's Mind Craft: what I'm building is lit.
P.R.E.V.A.I.L is a lifestyle and culture,
so you know it's legit.
Frustrated at times so I wanted to quit.
Had things organized but wasn't fully equipped.
My creativity is out of this world.
Far from cocky but I know that I'm thorough.
I could do anything I put my mind to.
That's the power of the mind just to remind you.
Keep working on your craft that's muscle memory.
Keep painting them pictures displaying imagery.
Continue creating your pieces of art
so the world could see its symmetry.

For You and All Youth

Please continue to be a great kid
and give live your very best.
Some tests you will pass and some tests you will fail.
It's all a learning lesson to help you PREVAIL.
Continue to observe and give your very all.
Life will knock you down many times, just ignore the fall.
Most importantly, get back up and stand up tall.
Please never give up nor quit.
Stay hungry and display true grit.
Remember to be disciplined, determined, and dedicated.
Success is that seed you plant
which will grow as you become more educated.
Your mind will be elevated,
and all of your hard work will be celebrated.
Make yourself and family proud.
You will soon be an adult in this world
and no longer a child.
You will take on many responsibilities
and be a helping hand.
This is for you and all youth who will one day
understand.

The End

We at the end of the book
almost the last page.
I used to always hear momma say,
"it's the last dayz"
I was young at the time,
so I thought it was a phrase.
Now our brains shackled
 while we're stuck inside a maze.
I P.R.E.V.A.I.L in this life
as I planted all my seeds.
This the time now
that we see all prophecies
and even false prophets.
The alarm on with no snooze button
so we can't stop it.
I do God's work to help uplift my people.
We up against the evil.
Love, Pain, and Glory
So here's the sequel.
Writing all my scriptures
while still looking through the peek hole.
If you really know me
then you know I have a deep soul
Last shot and 1
so I need my free throw.

Break Up 2 Make Up

Listen up, I promise to pick up when you call.
I apologize for the past and all the writings on the wall.
No lip-service involved but we dropped the call.
I needed Wi-Fi, matter 'a' fact, correct that—
I needed Wi-Fe.
You good with them tricks so you know how to excite me.
Brain out of this world every time you open your mouth,
you enlighten me.
I stare right into your eyes, baby, you're so exquisite.
Listen to me speak and see how my words are so vivid.
Poetic tongue got you cumming just to revisit.
Passionate love will make you want to re-live it.

Most High

If our leaders are killed then we kill the youth.
I made my own Blueprint filled with the truth.
I left my own seeds, so your 3rd eye could see.
I created it straight from scratch, so it's all me.
All the brain storming paid off through the years.
Struggle hurt us so badly that we're immune to the tears.
Everybody has a story that needs to be shared.
Ups and downs made it easy to see who cared.
In life, you can choose to be loved or be feared.
Everybody's stories are scriptures to be read.
Everybody had that thought "what if I were dead."
We were all given life since the umbilical cord.
Despite any issues always give special thanks to the Lord.
Divine status thinking is deeper than "I"
Be woke to understand—
that's the Most High.

Blessings

Count your blessings every time when you wake up.
Keep your circle tight like bricks so it's hard to break up.
If you don't, then that's an easy way to lose friends.
Handle business first, that's how you tie loose ends.
They say the proof is in the pudding, but it all depends.
Think about how we live and what's happening.
We saw many things change from over the years.
Caught us off guard even when we felt prepared.
We felt the flash in the moment as it just happened fast.
Catch your dreams, don't chase it.
The Meek Shall inherit the Earth.
Receive the blessings and embrace it.

Real Recognize Real

I get so many compliments on how I'm raising my son.
It puts a smile on my face, but I know the job not done.
Honestly daddy duties for me is like a hobby.
I aim to be perfect, yes, I'm talking Godly.
When it comes to being a parent,
I'm trying to perfect my craft.
I feel like a top pick entering the draft.
I know I'll go undrafted,
so I promise to make those who passed up on me pay.
Actions speak louder than words,
but I still write what I will like to say.
Can't expect things to always go your way so take it day-by-day.
It's just like a scar which takes time to heal.
Don't expect to be acknowledged all the time
but when you are,
understand that Real Recognize Real.

20/20 Vision

Praying to God is my daily devotion.
Try not to get caught up in your emotions.
Keep grinding and you might get a promotion.
My words so deep- they're deeper than the ocean.
Rhyme after rhyme, I'm stimulating minds like doing a line
Commit a crime? you better be willing to do the time.
Growing up now you see every sign.
You saw it young, but you were probably acting blind.
2020 is here, this could be the year.
Started off rough and it had us all scared.
I know the whole world at one point this year has shed a tear.
20/20 vision is clear to see how you're living.
Helping hand so what do you consider giving?
Ticking clock with Black Lives Matter Movement
so it's time for a Buy Back the Block Movement.
Stay focused and don't stop.
New Year hit and I hope you're achieving one or all of your goals before the next ball drop.
Don't forget to appreciate all that you got.
Cold summer but 2020 could be a global warming for a winter that's hot.
I was young but I remember trying to figure out why it's called 20/20 News
I guess it was predicting what's going to happen in the year of 2020 with many clues.
I was ahead of my time, but the oppressors will always be steps ahead.
3rd eyes opened wide in 2020 all due to someone being dead.
Resurrection and change coming so I already made up my bed.
Left messages through my words
To be cherished and read.
Making strategic moves but only a chosen few know why I fled.
I'm giving you Love, Pain, and Glory
so please don't let it go over your head.
Come to me if you can for any feelings you have instead of going over my head.
I hope to touch all my loved ones and peers.
2020 is a year that we grow from the Last Tears.

The Last Tears

Love, Pain, and Glory:
The Last Tears.
I've been jogging around in circles.
I've been running up and down the stairs.
I've been walking back and forth.
As if a baby is about to appear.
I've been losing lots of sleep.
I've sowed what I reaped.
I've rebuked any defeat.
This might be my last run when it comes to poetry.
Hip-Hop feel from Love, Pain, and Glory.
I'm all cried out from sharing my journey and all of my story.
Best believe, I still have a conscience.
Still have a sense of humor and could be obnoxious.
To truly understand you have to really know me.
Don't keep all your tears bottled in.
Open up and let them free.
As well as all of your fears throughout the years
Love and Blessings from me to you:
The Last Tears!

Made in the USA
Columbia, SC
15 November 2020